I Fancy Myself a Writer

Kyle A. Nelson

BookLeaf Publishing

Presentation by *BookLeaf Publishing*

Web: www.bookleafpub.com

E-mail: info@bookleafpub.com

ISBN: 9789357215428

First edition 2022

To my daughter, Celia.

ACKNOWLEDGEMENT

A sincere thank you to my family, my friends, and whatever forces that exist in our infinite universe that conspired to give me this opportunity.

I Fancy Myself a Writer

From sales floor and worksites to factories
Hands at work creating and changing
Mouth at work convincing and pandering
All the while a nagging itch remains below
The desire to not just be a marless cog
Sometimes called just seeking attention
Told just enough that I can chase these dreams
Fingers stretching above blue cotton and oil
Grasping tight at that sword-striking quill
Ignorance muddying those first strokes
But all muscles grow with use
And the foreign becomes naturalized
Whatever mettle may be untested
Benchmarks, touchstones not reached
That's all true and I don't deny, but still
I fancy myself a writer.

A Rusty, Two-Sided Coin

I admit that I don't understand my own heart
The conflicting passions that flitter about
One day desiring to bring all to everyone
To spread that light refusing to be hid
And this is the me that loves so much
This is the one that can do it all with a smile
Though he never seems to accomplish much
He holds up what he cannot build himself
That task falls to the one who cannot look out
The one inside who wishes to be alone
The one who can create works of substance
Never choosing to be the one who labors
With a desire only to do what must be done
It is from the depths that we build a ladder
Reaching to those heights of gaiety and mirth

An Ineffable Bit of Blah

I guess I want to be understood.
I want to be wanted.
I want to be needed.
There's something else though, something I can't quite name.
It feels like I want a friend.
It feels like I want reassurance that I haven't ruined everything.
I'm afraid to admit that I'm aching. That there's this nagging pain.
I want to be strong. I want to be unbreakable.
I want to admit I'm scared. I want to admit I need someone.
There's a void, or maybe it's a lack of depth.
There's a pit of gray nothing that's no deeper than a puddle.
I don't know. The words are there, but I can't build them.

Remember Your Love

Remember your Love
Remember your Joy
When the days are long
And life is a blur

There will be hard times
It won't be easy
But it must be done
You have to do it

You do have the strength
Hold on to these drives
Remember your Joy
Remember your Love

Green, Orange, and Yellow

There's something about the last and first days
The strange, confusing mix of life and death
The emerald green that clings from one
And the orange and yellow that beckon another
It's a place where you can feel the tears shed
And all the laughs that stole your breath away
It's a time when everything was at its best
Right before everything became the worst
But it's a change that must happen
It is the birthing pains and release of death
That sign of existence letting go
Yet all we wish to do is cling tighter
The ancients celebrated and had festivals
Creating myths to explain why this happens
When half the world lies in mourning
Unable to see the other and the first signs of life
It's a place I go when I'm seeking the past
And hoping for a view into the future
It's a scene that tells me it's time to move on
And reminds me that it will not be easy
It's a thing dying and must be removed
It's memories that can be painful
Looking at all the happy times
It's a chance to say goodbye
And the warmth of hello.

It's funny.

Huh.
It's funny.
Writing with a greasy pen,
with all this constant noise around me?
Not at all easy to think.
But to call myself
a writer?
Yes.

Emily

They call it
Hope, a thing.
A feeling.
She called it
feathered, and
says it sings.
Perches in
all our souls.
That few storms
could stop it.
She was right.
Hope will sing
the Heart's tune,
and won't ask
for a crumb.

The Lunar Sonnet

Your little siblings have been called diamonds
You have the shining beauty of a pearl
And which you value higher can depend
Twinkling little gems to your gorgeous swirls
You are the caring angel who watches
The constant vigil over us below
Even when your face is hidden in shade
You return with the same comforting glow
A sure guide for us in the darkest times
A shining promise of Day's return
The warming embrace of a kind lover
You are the promise of Hope high above
Forever my friend, My Luna, My Love

The Roll of the Dice

I say it's fun
To spend time with my friends
Us, sitting around the table
Just enjoying each other's company
The game is just an excuse to get together
But the laughs, the memories are all real and I
could not ask for anything more.

Aggressively Optimistic.

Aggressively
Optimistic
That's what it's called
It's how we fight
To make today
Even brighter
Than yesterday
And tomorrow
A shining light

Whistling While I Work

Whistling while I work
Is an old habit
Can't remember when
I even started

A lot of people
Just can't stand the sound
But I just can't help
Whistling while I work

The days are all long
And the weeks are short
But I will still keep
Whistling while I work

Shall I teach her to
Whistle while she works
Or to find something
Where she won't have to

I whistle at work
Because it helps me
Get through the long hours
That seem to drag by

Artificial lights
Loud machinery
All 'round but I'll keep
Whistling while I work

Trying to make smiles
And old memories
For us both, I'll keep
Whistling while I work

Ode to a Good Boss

As much as men are loathe to admit it
And some will tell you one does not exist
There are some adept at keeping spirit
Whose presence and temperament would be
missed
Despite the groans, there can be a good boss
Who keeps his men more loyal than good pay
And if the system takes them, it's a loss
Because they treat their men well come what
may
They can make a tough job bearable
And even make a hard job worth the pain
Their men know their boss is reliable
And from poor behaviors they will refrain
So treat a good boss well until they're gone
And for the new boss? Try and get along.

Man is Made to Work

Man is made to struggle
To work for his comfort
And for those that he loves

Frankly, he's made to work
To labor in the Sun
Feeling sweat on his brow

For this work his soul yearns
To find meaning in it
To realize his full worth

His work is part of him
Will even mark his soul
Like it will mark his hands

From the hunter of old
With crude bone and stone tools
Who must kill for his part

To the tired worker
In stores and factories
Who labor for money

All men are made to work

Creating his value
In what he gives away

Man is a Writer

Man is a writer
Seeing the threads everywhere
A storyteller

From how his day goes
To the birth of the cosmos
He writes about it

Building the story
Fitting together pieces
Solving mysteries

Finding the reasons
For all his sorrows and joys
His struggles to steer

Man needs his stories
HIs fantasy, his fable
So he keeps writing

It Ain't That Bad of a Day

It ain’t that bad of a day
It may be raining
And I do have to work late
And go to the store
But it ain’t that bad of a day

I saw a rainbow today
Laughed at a good joke
And talked with the cute cashier

It ain’t that bad of a day
The house is empty
And all my friends are busy
I have no plans tonight
But it ain’t that bad a day

I can catch up on some chores
And finish laundry
Finish that book I’m reading

It ain’t that bad a day
I really think so
After all, I’ve got my health
And not too much stress
So it ain’t that bad a day

Do you know?

If it's my youth
It will pass
If it's cowardice
It will pass
But
If it's my heart
It won't stop
If it's my calling
It won't stop
So
What do we do?
Do you know?
What are we meant for?
Do you know?

Ballad of the Starseekers

How far and fast they flit away
Your small, little children
Dust and ash, molded from your clay
Now scattered on the wind

Leaving your heart in their hands
Brave little explorers
Going to those strange, far-off lands
Unsatisfied watchers

They leave with barely a look back
Unafraid of the void
And you struggle not to lose track
As they dodge asteroids

You wonder how far they will go
Wanting them to be great
Nervous to see them go alone
What changes will they make

From star to star, they'll hop, ageless
And you left with the years
They're so very young and restless
And you holding back tears

How do you console a sad mother
Who watches her kids leave
Can’t share the pain with another
So you must let her grieve

Food and Stories

The two most human acts
Centered around sharing
Our souls full of kindness
Full of love and awe
Before large monuments
Before we went to space
We cooked for each other
We told each other stories
And often, they paired
Oft' used together
Improving each one
Bettering each other
Much as we do ourselves

Thanks, Mom

When you wish to thank someone
For an unpayable debt
For things they have given you
That are utterly priceless
What are the right words?

How do you say to someone
Things you barely understand
Life long emotions
Growing over years
How do you begin?

To thank a mother for love
For the countless healing words
The comforting, home cooked meals
And for everything else
That can't be paid back.

Not that you would ever ask
You were the one who taught me
About generosity
And showing love to others
Taught me to be kind

There are a million other

Lessons you showed me back then
And I thought I learned it all
Every little trick you had
Boy, How I was wrong.

I can't thank you enough, Mom
No matter how hard I try
I know you never measured
Or tried to count up the cost
So I'll give you what I can
And end with an, "I love you."

An Honest Limerick

I ain't never had too much beat
Must have been born with two left feet
So don't take the chance
I really can't dance
You are much safer in your seat

A True Story

Born on the banks of the winding Ohio
To a young girl who was just seventeen
Raised on the ruins of what used to be the west
But to see the open plains was his dream

He grew up and watched the future move to the stars
And he found himself dreaming of the moon
Singing her love songs during all the sleepless nights
Thinking tomorrow could not come too soon

Until he saw something of even more beauty
His heart was stolen by a little girl
His future was full of visions of golden hair
Before he knew it, she was his whole world

Now he dreams about what her tomorrows will be
And how he can give her everything
He still pictures the open plains and the bright stars
But more important is giving her wings

www.ingramcontent.com/pod-product-compliance
Lightning Source LLC
Chambersburg PA
CBHW051756130826
49812CB00033B/1183
9789357215428